The gang is in New Orleans for Mardi Gras, so it is guaranteed that they will see a ghost. Sure enough, in the water park next to the cemetery, two Civil War ghosts, Jed and Caleb Leland, chase after them. Find Scooby-Doo, Shaggy, Fred, Daphne, and Velma and help them escape the Leland Brothers.

Scooby-Doo

Velma

Fred

Shaggy

Daphne

Caleb Leland

Jed Leland

The gang finds out that the Mystery Machine once belonged to the Mystery Kids band! When the van starts acting weird, they take it to their mechanic, Murph. At the shop, they find out that Murph has been acting weird, too. In Murph's private office, there is a Mystery Kids shrine. Look for these Mystery Kids things to help solve the mystery.

Mystery Kids night-light

Mystery Kids lunch box

Mystery Kids alarm clock

Mystery Kids record album

Mystery Kids lamp

Mystery Kids T-shirt

Mystery Kids board game

The gang goes to Las Vegas to catch a concert, but the ghost of Rufus Raucous is trying to sabotage it. But wait! The real Rufus Raucous is alive and well and sabotages the ghost with his famous tricks. Look for these magical things.

Pack of cards

Top hat

Floating bottle

Magic scarf

Dove box

Linking rings

Sword box

Scooby! Scooby-Doo, where are you? All the animals in the jungle have gone ape. They are wild and glowing, and Scooby is among them. Help solve the mystery by looking for these animals in their altered states.

Scooby

Jocko

Lion

Leopard

Zebra

Gorilla

Rhinoceros

While shopping for a gift, Scooby, Shaggy, Fred, Daphne, and Velma find that the toys aren't playing around when they come to life in the toy store. Stay with the gang after the mall closes and help them uncover the real mystery by finding these subversive toys.

Battleship

G.I. Steve

Paratrooper

Jeep

Tank

Soldier

Bomber

While Scooby and the gang vacation in Italy, they hear about the ghost of a gladiator who lived when Mt. Vesuvius erupted the first time in 79 A.D. The meddling bambinos go to Pompeii to investigate and discover that the volcano might erupt again! Help solve the mystery by finding these ancient artifacts in the piles of garbage.

Helmet

Vase

Pot

Candelabra

Bracelet

Sculpture

Painting

The gang wins a contest to meet Luis Santiago, who is trying to break the all-time home run record. After the introductions, they become acquainted with a ghost who throws flaming heat at Luis to keep him from reaching his goal. Help the gang discover the mystery of the fiery fastballs.

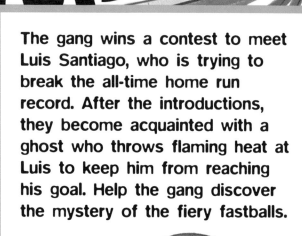

Regular baseballs

Fire extinguisher

Bucket of sand

Matches

Gasoline

Kerosene

Pail of water

Go back to the tank room at the Space Center and look for the janitor's undercover cleaning supplies.

_____ Eavesdrop mop

_____ Zoom broom

_____ Giveaway spray

_____ Tracks wax

_____ Hush brush

_____ Microscope soap

Go back to the water park and help Daphne find her spare shoes that were scattered in the chase.

_____ True shoe

_____ Blue shoe

_____ Moo shoe

_____ Glue shoe

_____ Flew shoe

_____ Cuckoo shoe

Go back to Murph's private office and look for evidence of his other hobbies.

_____ Coin collection

_____ Stamp collection

_____ Origami

_____ Needlepoint

_____ Accordion

_____ Golf clubs

Go back to Las Vegas and help Rufus and the gang understand the gravity of the situation by finding these clues.

_____ Scooby's collar

_____ Fred's keys

_____ Shaggy's belt buckle

_____ Daphne's compact

_____ Velma's watch